Standing

on the

Promises

Defeating Fear and Breaking Barriers

Alton E. Sumner

Broad Wing Press

Standing on the Promises

© Alton E. Sumner

© Broad Wing Press

ISBN: 978-1-938373-93-0

LCCN: 2024950033

Table of Contents

Dedication i

Foreword ii

Introduction 1

One – Foundation 5

Two – Fear 14

Three – Faith 21

Four – Hope 30

Five – Barriers 43

Six – Daddy 50

Seven – Resilience 63

Eight – Mama 71

Nine – Promises 78

Ten – Love 88

Conclusion 94

About the Author 103

Dedication

This book is dedicated to my dad, Pastor Jesse Eugene Sumner, Sr., and my mom, Mrs. Lillie Belle Davis Sumner, who would have been ecstatic to see the fulfillment of so many divine promises in my life. It is also dedicated to three people who pushed me to put my story in writing. Bishop Alfred Owens, Jr., who was my pastor for more than thirty-three years, began urging me to write this book about four years ago and has checked in frequently to make sure I was working on it. My friend and fellow minister, Dr. Barbara Reynolds, has been a driving force, constantly encouraging me to write it. And my wife, Betty, simply would not let me quit.

Foreword

It is both an honor and a privilege to have been asked to write the foreword for this wonderful work, *Standing on the Promises*, from the heart of Reverend Doctor Alton Sumner. This book is more than a collection of thoughts—it is an anthology of Rev. Sumner's weekly messages that have brought hope and encouragement to so many. Originally, these were sent to leaders in the sick and shut-in ministry, and various other members of the Greater Mt. Calvary Holy Church congregation who were walking through difficult seasons. These messages were designed to uplift those in need of prayer, remind them of the power of God's promises, and encourage them to continue trusting Him even when life's circumstances seemed bleak.

What makes *Standing on the Promises* so powerful is its deeply personal nature. Sumner draws from his own life, growing up in rural North Carolina, to share stories of hardship, perseverance, and faith. His transparency about his trials during adolescence and early adulthood offers readers a glimpse into the formative experiences that shaped his unwavering trust in God. Through his reflections, we are reminded that no matter what we face, God's promises remain steadfast.

When I first read these messages, I was struck by Sumner's unique ability to blend wit and wisdom with genuine humility. His words feel like a warm embrace, gently guiding the reader to a place of peace and reassurance in God's faithful promises. It wasn't long before I encouraged him to compile these messages into this book, believing that they would bless many beyond the walls of our church. I am confident that this is only the beginning of what Sumner has to offer, and that there are more powerful episodes of faith, hope, and encouragement yet to come.

As you read *Standing on the Promises*, allow yourself to be drawn into the heart of the author and you will find yourself inspired by his wisdom, touched by his honesty, and reminded that no matter the trials you face, God is faithful to fulfill His promises. Whether in need of encouragement or seeking to strengthen your faith, this book will speak to your heart in profound ways.

So, as you journey through these pages, take time to reflect on the lessons, savor the wisdom, and above all, be reminded that God's promises are sure and stand the test of time. May this beautiful collection inspire you to continue standing on the unshakable promises of God.

Archbishop Alfred A. Owens, Jr., D. Min.
Founding Pastor, Greater Mount Calvary Holy Church
Washington, D. C.

Introduction

My heart pounded harder with each buzz, as I waited for my big brother, Jesse Jr., to answer his phone. I silently wondered if his voice would be downcast. Should I infiltrate his grief? Was it too soon to engage him in conversation? How would I even begin the discourse?

Jesse Jr. had been battling pancreatic cancer for nearly a year when his wife, Deloris, became severely ill. Deloris was my first "sister-in- love." She had been a part of our family since I was thirteen and lived in our home during most of my teenage years. When, as a young teenager, I was bitten by a vicious dog and ran home bleeding, Deloris dressed my wound. When my family moved to Halifax in the last semester of my senior year in high school, Deloris and Jesse Jr. allowed me to move into their house in Enfield with them to avoid changing schools so close to graduation. So it seemed that Deloris had always been there. But my brother's life-long companion would not survive this illness.

As difficult as the news of her passing was for me, I was concerned that the greater pain my brother felt might cause him to surrender the fight for his health, and I had no idea how to encourage him. Still, the morning after Deloris transitioned to heaven, I called. Jesse answered on the third ring with the greeting he often extended when answering my call. *"Hey-y-y, Alton!"* This signaled to me that he was glad I had called and that the cold hand of death that snatched his dearest friend had not seized the buoyant spirit he needed to continue his fight. Still, I struggled to find words to comfort and encourage him. My big brother could clearly discern my quandary, came to *my* rescue, and took over the conversation. Paraphrasing the words of King David after the death of his infant son, he calmly affirmed, *"I will go to her, but she will not return to me. In the meantime, the work God has for me must continue and I can't do it by sitting around languishing in despair. She is in heaven and my work, for now, is here"* (2 Sam 12:23).

With this, Jesse Jr. assured me that he was okay. There really wasn't anything I needed to say, for my concern in checking on him had been enough. In the middle of a fiery trial in which his wife was gone, and his health was deteriorating, he accepted his bitter cup and resolved to complete his mission as pastor of the Royal Light Church of Deliverance. At Deloris' homegoing service, he took a microphone his daughter Linda passed to him and sang, *"I made it! I made it out alright!"* And for the next year, he persevered in the work God had given him.

Although he had been known for spirited preaching and inspirational singing that motivated, challenged, and endeared his audiences, he was no longer able to stand for any length of time. He delivered his final sermon and song from a chair beside the pulpit. His voice, was still strong and steady as he intoned with perfect tonal quality,

The road is rough and the going gets tough,
The hills are hard to climb.
I started out a long time ago,
And there is no doubt in my mind,
I've decided to make Jesus my choice!

For the last five years, I have been writing a weekly inspirational blog drawn primarily from my experiences growing up in the rural Jim Crow era South. In this collection of memories and life lessons, I share stories from my struggles, for we are products of our background and lived experiences. In following my divinely designed path and trusting in the Lord as Proverbs 3:5 instructs us), I have gleaned golden nuggets of wisdom from my experiences—that can help others discover and fulfill their God-ordained purpose.

It took a while to fully understand that executing my divine purpose was not solely for my benefit, but could ultimately benefit others as well. My father, a sharecropping farmer, and a savvy, witty, Holy Spirit-filled country preacher, used Scripture to teach me how to navigate the pitfalls of life. My mother was my first love and, until her death, I shared every major move, decision, and accomplishment with her. In this work, I have devoted a chapter to each of them.

The reluctant telephone call to my brother taught me that it is always the correct time to do what is necessary and right. The conversation drove home that we must never abandon our mission. And when our work is done, we must pass it on to the right person to continue. My nephew, Jesse Sherrod Sumner, was divinely chosen to assume leadership of the church his father had pastored for more than 40 years. In his waning years, Jesse, Jr. had groomed his son to assume the work.

There are times when we must drink from a bitter cup and travel a difficult road. But if we are faithful to the mission, God promises that we will rise triumphantly. Meta tauta," a Greek phrase John used in the book of Revelation, means "*after these things.*" For if we remain faithful to our divinely assigned mission through the difficult struggles we often endure, we will experience better times! I am grateful to God that after so many difficult times, I am living in my victorious meta-tauta season.

One
Foundation

"Standing on the promises of Christ my King. Through eternal ages let His praises ring."

Uncle FG

Golden sunlight graced the horizon on a brilliant spring Sunday morning in April of 1965. Ah-h, yes, 1965, the year the Voting Rights Act was passed. It safeguarded the rights of all citizens to vote without discriminatory qualifications such as literacy tests, and just one year earlier, the 1964 Civil Rights Act legally ended the Jim Crow era. The Vietnam War in Southeast Asia was heating up; Lyndon Johnson was being tested in his first year as the duly elected president of the United States. Alfred Owens, Jr., who decades later would have a profound impact on my life, was a teenager contemplating starting a storefront church in Washington, DC.

Meanwhile, brightly colored orange monarch and black swallowtail butterflies glided playfully through the yard behind our olive-green farmhouse on

Springhill Farm in Enfield, North Carolina, an archetypal southern town with a railroad track dividing the black and white residential areas. Genteel colonial, Victorian, and Elizabethan homes lined Franklin, Main, and Sherrod Heights streets on the white side, while modest shotgun-style houses were along Dixon, Dennis, and Pope Streets on the "other" side.

Dressed in my "Sunday-best" white shirt, red bowtie, black pants, and shoes freshly polished with Griffin Liquid Wax, I squeezed into the car with my dad, mom, and four siblings—16 year-old Gwendolyn, 13 year-old Griffin, and the four year-old twins, Denise and Venise, My oldest brother, Jesse, Jr., was at Army boot camp at Fort Jackson, South Carolina and my two oldest sisters, Helena and Louetta, were in college at North Carolina Central University in Durham. Since the twins, Denny and Neta, as we called them, were small, the seven of us fit into our six-seater 1958 Pontiac Chieftain for the twelve-mile ride through the countryside to the Royal Light Holiness Church of Deliverance in Tillery.

Tillery has a complex history. At one time, it had been a sprawling slave plantation. Then, in 1889, it was incorporated as a town in Halifax County. In the 1930s and 1940s, the vast 18,000 acres of farmland had become part of President Franklin Roosevelt's New Deal Resettlement Program—one of only fifteen such resettlement projects for African Americans nationwide. And in 1936, three years into Roosevelt's first term, the name of Tillery Resettlement Farm was changed to Roanoke Farms.

Farmers, who had been sharecropping the Tillery plantation since the Civil War ended in 1865, were given the opportunity to purchase farms on the property. My grandfather, Freeland Grandford Sumner, Sr., had migrated to North Carolina from Waycross, Georgia, around 1919 and worked his way up to become a foreman on sharecropping properties in Halifax County. In the 1940s, he purchased forty acres in Tillery's Crowell's community and a much larger farm (155 acres) in the northeastern Halifax area known as the Slashes Lowlands. To this day, both remain as properties of the Freeland Sumner, Sr. family.

The area was likely named Slashes Lowlands due to its location in the Roanoke River floodplain. Enforced segregation allowed white people to purchase property in the upper region of West Halifax. But black-owned farms were concentrated in the lower floodplain region around Caledonia Prison, the Conoconnara Swamp, Dawson, and Crowell's.

According to Resettlement Project plans, in addition to a main house, each farm was to have four additional structures—a barn, a hen house or chicken coop, a smokehouse, and an outhouse. For the first six years of my life, we lived on the farm that my grandfather had purchased in the Slashes Lowlands.

All these structures, except a smokehouse, were on the property. Our house did not have indoor plumbing. That convenience, at least in the early stages of the project, was reserved for the houses in west Halifax.

From as far back as I can remember, Tillery has always looked like a ghost town except for our church. Whatever businesses were there had long since moved on, and a trip there felt like a trip to *nowhere*. Twenty minutes after leaving home that Sunday morning, we pulled into the dirt yard of the wooden, white frame building that was the former Shady Grove School.

The Hawkins sisters, a family in our church, had purchased the school building, which my grandfather converted into a house of worship. The sisters, who were all school teachers, joined Royal Light when the church was still meeting in family homes for Sunday services and Friday night prayer meetings.

Inside the sanctuary that had been the auditorium, I fixed my eyes on the slender gentleman with caramel brown skin and a slowly receding hairline as he stood behind the small oakwood table in the front. With his hands stretched toward the congregation, he motioned for us to stand, then led us in singing *"Standing on the Promises of God"*—our unofficial Sunday School anthem,

> *Standing on the promises of Christ my king*
> *Through eternal ages let His praises ring.*
> *Glory in the highest I will shout and sing!*
> *I am standing on the promises of God.*

My uncle, Freeland Grandford Sumner, Jr., affectionately known as Uncle FG or Uncle F, had been our Sunday School teacher since as far back as I could remember. At eleven years of age, that felt like a long time. He and my dad, the Sunday School superintendent, had been forced by the harsh, unsympathetic demands of farm life to end their formal schooling much too soon. Still, they never stopped reading purposefully, observing sharply, and thinking critically—NEVER—for as long as they were alive and breathing! They were *life-long learners.* Though familial relationships tend to cause us to be somewhat biased, I view them as two of the savviest men I have known.

When Uncle F, who was four years older than my dad, was born in 1916, Woodrow Wilson was the president of the United States. Although he is remembered for starting the League of Nations (forerunner of the United Nations), presiding over the ratification of the nineteenth amendment, giving women the right to vote, and appointing the first Jewish member of the Supreme Court, he had a bully pulpit, and he openly supported the Ku Klux Klan in his five-volume history textbook, *A History of the American People* in 1902. Even the president, whose responsibility was the welfare of all the citizens of the country, could be racist.

At that time, though one-third of North Carolina's school-aged population was black, there were no public high schools for black children. So, as young black men, barriers to education and employment limited Uncle F and my dad's opportunities for social and economic advancement. Yet, while both were under 50 that year, they had garnered a wealth of experience leading up to that April Sunday morning.

My dad was 45, and Uncle F was 49. When he turned 50, Uncle F often reminded us, "I'm half-a-hundred." Though today, that is considered the prime of life, in 1965, the life expectancy for black males was 61 years, and neither Dad nor Uncle F would live to see 60.

Uncle F was a no-nonsense gentleman who would, without a moment's hesitation, put anyone in check if they disrespected him by using coarse language or attempted to tell obscene jokes. He loved teaching Sunday school and would often pause while reading a particular verse, place a forefinger to his cheek, raise an eyebrow, look straight at us, and assert, *"There is a sermon in that!"* or as church folk say nowadays, *"That'll preach!"* Then, as he pounded the point, he would chuckle and exclaim, *"The devil don't like nothin' like this!"*

From the deacon's corner, the affirmation, *"Make it plain! Say so Deacon!"* would inevitably be voiced by Deacon Frank Shelly, a Rocky Mount businessman to whom Uncle F had "witnessed," shared the gospel and invited to the church when it was still meeting in our living room on second Sundays and Uncle F's living room on fourth Sundays.

In those days, churches in the south met on either first and third or second and fourth Sundays. This provided an opportunity to attend and support other churches on Sundays. Little Zion Baptist, pastored by Reverend Cotton, was within walking distance of our house. We also visited Plumbline United Holy Church, pastored by Elder Young, in the Enfield countryside, and Walter's Chapel Holiness Church, pastored by Elder Lynch in Hollister. We often frequented big singing events at Ivory Hill Baptist Church in Hollister, pastored by Elder Copeland.

Visiting those churches had benefits beyond being a place to worship on Sundays. As my brothers and I came into adolescence, we couldn't help but notice all those pretty girls! Jesse Jr. met and fell in love with Deloris, a member of Walter's Chapel. Elder Copeland officiated at their wedding in the spring of 1967. My first cousin, Simon Justice, met his wife at Ivory Hill.

As I grew older, whenever I had the opportunity to ride with Uncle F and glean from his wit and wisdom, I felt strongly that if racial and socioeconomic barriers were not so entrenched, he might have been a lawyer, doctor, or a professional educator. He might have become a college professor like Thomas Sewell Inborden, the black man from the mid-west who established Brick Junior College in Enfield in 1895. Mr. Inborden was the first principal of that prestigious school from which my mother graduated in 1942. By then, however, racism had forced this private college to shut down, and it had become a public high school under white control. Yet, this historic institution remained a strong academic school served by many of the same teachers who had served the junior college.

Uncle F did not just teach Sunday School; he lived it and loved it! And he *loved his students* so much that he pushed us beyond merely **knowing** the lesson to **understanding** it. His unverbalized attitude was *hearing* is good and *knowing* is better, but *internalizing what you learn and putting it into practice* is best. His visible, if unspoken, attitude was, *"Don't just sit there and gaze at me, but* **understand this!"** His often repeated phrase or question was, "You get me now?"

> *Understand, therefore, that the LORD your God is indeed God. He is the faithful God who keeps his covenant for a thousand generations and lavishes his unfailing love on those who love him and obey his commands.*
>
> *Deut. 7:9 NLT*

Uncle F knew that such understanding would lead to perfect faith in God. Those scriptures in which he saw so many sermons were about the One he knew and believed was the only true and living God. He wanted us to **understand** that people would let us down or fail us, but if we loved and obeyed God with perfect faith, we could always stand on his wonderful promises! So, we sang:

Standing on the promises that cannot fail.
Though the howling storms of doubt and fears assail,
Through the living word of God, I shall prevail.
I am standing on the promises of God.
Standing! Standing! I am standing on the promises of God!

The direction of my life was established in church and rooted in lessons like the ones I learned in Uncle F's Sunday School class. Singing this hymn was an affirmation of faith through which we could face and ultimately defeat fear. It assured me that whatever path my life would take, I would always have beneath my feet a stable and secure **foundation**.

Two
Fear

When I was in the sixth grade at T. S. Inborden School, my curiosity peaked about the white school within approximately two miles walking distance of our house. Though my family lived on the mostly white side of the tracks at the edge of Enfield's city limits, it was owned by town commissioner Harry Branch. For my first five-and-a-half years of school, I was bussed to a school on the other side of the railroad tracks, more than twice the distance of the all-white school. So, I jumped at the opportunity to participate in an integration experiment implemented within deeply divided, severely segregated Halifax County.

The dual system of bussing white children to their schools and black children to separate schools had been the norm throughout North Carolina and much of the nation. Even after the Supreme Court rendered its 1954 *Brown v. Board of Education of Topeka, Kansas,* decision declaring that segregated schools were unconstitutional, race-based bussing continued in most school districts. Three years later, as more school districts attempted to carry out the Court's desegregation order, protests broke out in several cities.

After a 1971 decision by the North Carolina high court in a case, *Swann v. Charlotte-Mecklenburg Board of Education* upheld bussing for desegregation. The practice became a politically charged powder keg.

In 1977, after I obtained my first position as a social studies teacher, I took a group of students from Hillside High in Durham, North Carolina, to a forum on Capitol Hill entitled *"Bussing, Cussing, What's all the Fussing?"* one of several activities sponsored by the "Close-Up" Foundation for high school students. While sitting in that session, it struck me as ironic that bussing to achieve integration was so controversial and politically inflamed. Those who were shouting so angrily now had not raised so much as a whimper during the many decades that children like me had been bussed for racial separation.

Linda Brown's family had raised the bussing issue when, after having to walk six blocks to take the bus to Topeka's all-black elementary school, she attempted to enroll in the all-white Sumner Elementary School seven blocks from her home. Brown's situation was my situation. The school she attempted to enter even had my name! Though one of the candidates pursuing the presidency in 2024 asserted the United States has never been racist, black children throughout the nation have lived with this reality for more than a century.

There are various components to racism, and

unfounded fear of the unknown looms large among them. Yet, the Bible tells us that *"He who fears has not been made perfect in love"* (1 John 4:18 NKJV).

Fist Fight in Black and White

In the mid-1960s, the Halifax County Public Schools district's experimental "Freedom of Choice" school desegregation plan was a move to avoid losing federal funds under Title VI of the 1964 Civil Rights Act. Since it was highly unlikely that any white family would elect to have their children attend a "black school," the plan implicitly meant that black children who were willing to take the risk could opt to attend a "white school." In May of 1967, at the end of my sixth-grade school year at T. S. Inborden, when I was twelve years old, I informed my parents that I wanted to transfer to Enfield Graded School to begin junior high.

Junior or middle high school has been mockingly referred to as "the range of the strange" or "the herd of the absurd. It is the phase in the child's social and physical development in which they possibly experience the most phenomenal changes of their lives. During this period, bullying is often rampant. Add the racial tension of the time, and you have a sense of what I was about to walk into.

My parents knew it would be difficult, but my first cousin, Joyce Sumner, had already enrolled at Enfield Graded when "Freedom of Choice" was first implemented a few years earlier. And despite the ugliness of prejudice and racial discrimination, she stayed. So, they supported my decision, and that fall, I began a cultural experience that would further define the person I was destined to become. In the entire seventh grade that year, there were just four Black students: Reginald Johnson, Carlton Solomon, my cousin Hazel Irene Sumner, who was Joyce's younger sister, and me.

When I arrived at Enfield Graded School in August, I was greeted by fear in the faces and voices of the white children who shouted racial epithets at me. This fear undoubtedly had been cultivated in their homes. The words of the Marvin Gaye classic, "What's Going On," are reflective of what was going through my mind:

> Don't punish me with brutality
> Talk to me
> So you can see... Mother, mother...
> What's going on? What's going on?

One day, after being punched in my sides and back, badgered, and called contemptuous names for days, I faced my tormentor and demanded he stop taunting and attacking me. The big bully just laughed snidely and challenged me to a lunchtime fight between the gym and the mobile classrooms that housed the junior high school.

To my surprise, when I showed up, so did what appeared to be the entire seventh and eighth-grade classes. But despite the size of the crowd and the noise they made, no teacher or staff member showed up! The rambunctious multitude looked like the riotous group that stormed the nation's Capital 53 years later, on January 6, 2021.

I was tired of being picked on and called n----r and all I wanted was to be treated with respect. If it took going to blows with this bully to get it, I was willing. But my antagonist stood head and shoulders above me, and I had no illusions of being able to beat him! Yet, fed up with his racist bullying, I felt compelled to take a stand.

After sustaining several blows to my head and landing punches against my much taller opponent wherever I could, the atmosphere grew increasingly tense. Suddenly, a girl—the sister of one of the bully's friends—began crying and screamed at her brother. But he, along with several other boys, was busy hurling racist insults at me. Visibly shaken and disgusted by the appalling behavior of her brother and his mean-spirited companions, the girl's tearful protests finally brought the altercation to a halt. Still seething with anger, the bully and his friends warned me not to return to *their* school the next day, or they would be waiting with switchblade knives. This intimidation was a dastardly attempt to instill enough fear in me to provoke me to go whimpering back to the "black" school.

The fist fight that occurred near the middle of that

year reflected our treatment each day in that hostile environment. It was whispered that my white provocateur, who seemed to me to be too tall to be in the seventh grade, was repeating the grade for the third time. He wore a western-style belt and cowboy boots and was just plain mean. He wanted me to know how he felt about "n----s" attending *his* school. He sat behind me in the on-stage bleachers during seventh-grade choral practice.

After the lunchtime brawl, when the bell rang for class to begin again, there was a strange turn of events. The staff finally became involved. My seventh-grade teacher and another teacher called me outside to talk about the fight. They informed me that one of them had heard that *I had threatened* to bring a switchblade to school the next day and advised me that if this happened, I would be expelled. My side of the story seemed unimportant since neither asked to hear it. Nonetheless, I *was* in school the next day and heard nothing more from these two about the incident. Surprisingly, the fear my antagonists sought to impose on me had been replaced by a sense of peace and a calm, firm, and unwavering resolve to complete my secondary schooling at Enfield Graded School.

I did not share that incident with my parents for another year. Daddy would surely have gone to the school to see the principal if I had. He had previously met with him when I decided to attend the school and was treated with respect. Although I lived within walking distance of the school, the principal had offered to allow me to ride the school bus for safety. However, since the bus driver had not been informed of the arrangement and I was too afraid and embarrassed to try to explain that the principal had given his permission, I only rode the bus for one day. Neither my father nor the principal was aware of what happened after that incident. I walked to school on a route that led past the white cemetery and the "whites only" park. Though, occasionally, on that walk to or from school, I encountered bullies, the strong black men I looked up to had forged in me enough courage to face **fear.**

Three
Faith

"When the howling storms of doubt and fear assail, by the living word of God, I shall prevail."

Church

During its formative years, the church my grandfather founded had neither a building nor a name. It was just called *"Church,"* and at different times from 1946 until 1962, met in three Sumner family homes. Finally, my mother and older sisters, Helena, Louetta, and Gwendolyn, thought that though the church did not *yet* have an edifice, it should have a name. My mother suggested *"Royal Light,"* perhaps, because the church was where we felt closest to the One who is most **majestic** and the One who said, *"I am the **light** of the world. Whoever follows me will not walk in darkness but will have the light of life"* (John 8:12 ESV). After coming under the umbrella of the Deliverance Evangelistic Church organization in Philadelphia in the early 1960s, under Pastor Benjamin Smith, Sr., it became the Royal Light Church of Deliverance.

This church had a profound impact on me. Not only had my grandfather founded it and served as its first pastor, but my mother named the church that met in our living room each second Sunday, my uncle's home each fourth Sunday, and my grandfather's home each Friday night. Then my father became its third permanent pastor in 1967, and my oldest brother it's fifth in 1979.

> *"I pondered the direction of my life, and I turned to follow your laws."* (Ps 119:59 NLT)

Stepping out of the Light

At the end of my senior year in high school, my life took a turn when I moved away from my family and home church and lived on my own for the first time. It felt as if I was l stepping out of the light and wandering into the dark mystery of the unknown on the "big" college campus. As I prepared to leave home, I felt apprehensive as I remembered the experience of prejudice and fear at Enfield Graded. I had to choose between holding on to the faith values I had learned at home or running from my source of security and spiritual foundation.

When I arrived at North Carolina Central University in the "big" city of Durham, I *instinctively* began looking for people with a similar church connection. As if someone had taken my hand and begun leading me, I quickly discovered the Pentecostal

Fellowship Organization that provided me with a sense of family on campus.

Before leaving home, I attended a revival service in Rocky Mount, led by Pastor Mary Barnes. Despite not knowing me, after the service, she called me to the front and prophesied that I was destined to become a minister. Then she shocked me by saying, *"God wants you to read Proverbs 3:5-6."*

> *"Trust in the Lord with all thine heart and lean not unto thine own understanding. In all thy ways acknowledge him and he shall direct thy path"* (KJV).

This was the passage I had read for the first time a few days earlier and scribbled beside it, *"Beautiful!"* Her words struck me like a lightning bolt. Now, at NCCU, it was clear to me that God really was directing my paths.

The Serpent!

It was not that all I ever did was pray and read my Bible. Although I attended church on campus each Sunday and sang and traveled with the Pentecostal Fellowship Choir, I was not immune to the tactics of the devil. Satan, the enemy of God and humanity, is armed with weapons of mass distraction, and as the Apostle Paul said, *"I find then a law, that, when I would do good, evil is present with me"* (Rom 7:21 KJV).

In the early 1970s, Evangelist Carrie Hunter [Bolton], a family friend, was preaching a revival sermon at a remote country church in the woods of Garysburg, North Carolina, down a dirt road off the beaten path. As she approached a high point in her sermon, the entire congregation suddenly jumped up, erupted in a loud shout, and started climbing on the pews. Was it the Rapture? No!

As we worshipped together at the end of a hot summer day, a large serpent had slithered into the little, packed sanctuary! As this devil switched across the floor—just like he did in the Garden of Eden, brave *'devil can't do me no harm'* saints jumped up on the pews and screamed. But Uncle F ran *toward* the beast and began jumping up and down on its head with the hard heels of his shoes until he immobilized it. Then, I watched in amazement as he grabbed it by the tail, took it outside, and discarded it.

That night, I witnessed two different ways to respond to the frightening evil that, suddenly and unannounced, pops up in life. I could panic like the congregation did. Or, I could square off, face it bravely, and immobilize it. The image of my uncle jumping up and down on the serpent's head lives in my mind to this day. Whenever I find myself veering off course or thinking the worst because of sickness, stress, or depression, I recall his bravery, courage, and faith. This was a man who had the values and teachings of the church in him and confronted and subdued the fears of a whole congregation under his feet. When the serpent approached him and tried to bruise his heel, he confronted it, attacked it, and bruised its head, (Genesis 3:15 KJV) like Jesus did at Calvary!

Without saying a word, Uncle F taught me that though scary and evil matters, situations, or people come to frighten and bruise me, I must not lose control. I must not panic! I only need to follow God's laws, then look whatever devil confronts me in the face! Confront it; attack it and immobilize it!

The seeds planted in such lessons often require a lengthy cultivation period to grow into a fully developed product. What Uncle F's courage taught me has taken years to mature. For far too long, I was victimized by the spirit of fear. Because of this, I did not embrace my call to ministry until several *decades* after Pastor Barnes' prophecy. Normal fear can be useful in preventing us from doing foolish things. It warns us not to venture through a dark alley alone at night, get into a car with strangers, swim in a pond filled with crocodiles, or saunter through a venomous snake pit. But a *spirit* of fear is entirely different. It attacks the mind, prevents us from reaching our God-given potential, and diminishes our capacity to *love.*

Hitchhiking Angel!

As a teenager, when my father was pastor, one of my tasks was driving his blue Plymouth station wagon to transport members from rural areas to and from services. This responsibility took me on journeys through the countryside, often covering long distances for Sunday worship, prayer, and Bible study on Wednesday nights, youth services on Friday nights, frequent revivals, and occasional Saturday night services.

In the early seventies, a story circulated about a hitchhiker along country roads at night whose countenance was so peaceful and magnetic that you could not pass him without offering him a ride. Once inside the car, he would proclaim calmly and authoritatively, *"Jesus is soon to come,"* then suddenly and quietly disappear. Like the announcement to the shepherds in a peaceful field near the little town of Bethlehem the night Jesus was born, this proclamation was intended to be glad tidings and a fair warning.

Now, I was fine with picking up and dropping off church members, but driving home down long, dark, lonely roads through dark woods alone at night was terrifying since I thought that I might encounter the angel hitchhiker! Yes, I loved Jesus and sang in church, *"Oh, I long to see Him, look upon His face, there to sing forever, of His saving grace."* but I was afraid that an apparition might appear in the darkness and cause me to wreck my father's station wagon! A visible appearance of a heavenly being in church surrounded by family and friends would have been fine. But an EWD—"epiphany while driving"—held no appeal for me! So, fearing that I might see Jesus much sooner than

I *really* wanted to, I would speed through the countryside, eager to arrive safely back home.

A story my dad once told me helps illustrate my state of mind at the time. One night, while preaching about the joy and wonders of heaven, a fiery country preacher paused in his sermon to ask, *"How many of you want to go to heaven?"* When everyone except one man raised their hands, the preacher looked at him with a perplexed expression and asked, *"Sir, you don't want to go to heaven?"* The puzzled gentleman responded, *"Yes, yes, I do. But I thought you were trying to get a load together to go tonight."* Like that congregant, I wanted to see Jesus, but not yet!

In Sunday school, I learned about an angel who appeared to Zechariah, a priest in Jerusalem, while he was on duty in the temple. I could relate to him because, according to Luke, *"When Zechariah saw him, he was troubled, and fear fell upon him"* (Lk 1:12 NKJV). But the angel was bringing good news for Zechariah and his wife, Elizabeth. What if, like mine, his fear caused him to flee from the temple? He might have missed a providential, life-altering encounter and once-in-a-lifetime opportunity to talk face-to-face with someone who stands *"in the presence of God,"* (Lk 1:19 KJV*).* He would not have experienced the miracle of fathering a child who would become John the Baptist, the forerunner of Jesus Christ!

Whether or not the story of the hitchhiking angel in the countryside was true, I was tormented with fear while doing church work! Besides chauffeuring members, I was a church musician with my brother, Jesse, Jr., and often led praise and worship during the "devotional/testifying," part of the services. Though the congregation often sang, *"I'm a Soldier in the Army of the Lord... a sanctified soldier in the army of the Lord!"* I was a *terrified* soldier during those drives through the pitch-dark woods. I am not certain if my fear of seeing a hitchhiking angel was normal or the ungodly spirit of fear. In hindsight, it foreshadowed a pattern of paralyzing fears that held me back from embracing opportunities, taking bold risks, and speaking the truth when it mattered most. This realization has taught me to confront and overcome my fears, while embracing courage and faith to live a more purposeful life.

Those fears manifested as low self-esteem, anxiety over other's opinions of me, and self-doubt about my ability to complete a task. They whispered lies, making me feel inadequate and uncertain. They even stifled my ability to connect with others, rendering me silent in group conversations and hesitant to engage in casual chats.

Despite being raised in a loving home surrounded by supportive parents and siblings, and enveloped by a close-knit extended family, low self-esteem slipped into my young heart. It quietly found a foothold in my mind and began taking shape in my psyche and casting a shadow over my tender years. I would have been perpetually trapped in that state if it had not been for what had been deposited within my soul that prodded me to see the unseen. That 'something' was **FAITH**!

Four
Hope

"All night, all day, angels watching over me, my Lord!"

The Slashes Lowlands

Despite apprehension, my introduction to angels was one of my most pleasant memories. Like my siblings, I was born at home. It was a cold winter night when my family was preparing to move away from Nichols' Farm, where my grandfather, grandmother, and all their children and their families had lived and worked.

As the foreman for the property, "Grandpa," as we called him, used that position to learn about business matters and earn enough to purchase the two farms in Halifax. He moved onto the 40-acre farm in the Crowell's community, and my father and mother moved with their family to the 155-acre farm in the Slashes Lowlands two weeks after I was born. When I was about three years old, my mother taught me the first song I ever learned to sing:

"All night, all day, angels watching over me, my Lord!
All night, all day, angels keep on watching over me!"
I went in the valley, and I didn't go to stay,
Angels watching over me my Lord.
My soul got happy and I stayed all day.
Angels watching over me.

I haven't been to heaven, but I'm on my way,
Angels watching over me my Lord.
Walking with Jesus every night and every day,
And the angels keep watching over me, my Lord!

In later years, I learned another verse below:

You can accuse me, you can abuse me;
You can shut me out of your fold;
You can attack my body
But you can't touch my soul
Cause the angels keep watching over me!
All night, all day, the angels keep watching over me!

Those words to the song mama taught me to sing gave me *hope* and a feeling of being cared for, protected, and loved. They subconsciously pried open a window that allowed me to see a better future.

The farm was charming and picturesque, with acres of land for growing cotton, corn, peanuts, and tobacco and vast woodlands providing timber for firewood and poles for making haystacks, fences, and places to explore. An obscure eighteenth-century graveyard was secluded in one section of the woods, and a medium-sized fishpond was in another. There were several apple trees, a pear tree, a large muscadine grapevine, and a row of plum trees near the woods. Mama planted a lush garden with a variety of beans, cabbages, collard greens, mustard greens, turnip greens, yellow squash, pumpkins, sweet potatoes, white potatoes, watermelons, and other crops. We had two mules named Emma and Ida, a milk cow named Cozy, and another cow named Pinhorn because of her sharp horns. We never named the other animals.

My parents were property holders with no money. Despite all these rich resources, the farm was never prosperous. Clandestine forces worked overtime to ensure my family would always be poor as long as we owned the land we lived on. Just one ill-informed economic move, and we would lose the farm. We were too rich to qualify for welfare or food stamps but poor enough that we had to borrow money from a wealthy white entrepreneur to buy seeds, farm equipment, clothing, food, and other necessities.

We drew water for cooking, drinking, bathing, washing clothes, and scrubbing the floors from an old well in the backyard. Electricity was expensive, so we mostly used kerosene lamps for lighting. A large console radio provided entertainment when we came in from the fields and listened to shows like "Suspense," "Gunsmoke," "Johnny Dollar," and the syndicated Wayne Raney country music show. I can still recall the tease lines of two of our favorites: "Suspense— 'A tale well calculated to keep you in Suspense'" and "Gunsmoke — 'The first man they look for, and the last they want to meet.'"

On Sunday mornings, we woke up to Joe Louis Hunter's gospel show on WCEC/WFMA in Rocky Mount. This distant relative, in his early to mid-20s, had the best radio voice I had ever heard! There was no lazy, southern drawl like most Southern white people, nor broken English or Gullah Geechee dialect spoken by some black people in South Carolina and coastal North Carolina. His calming, deep, melodious tone and perfect diction introduced the popular gospel recording groups, always identifying their home city, after migrating away from the South in most cases. He would say things like, "Up next, we've got The Dixie Hummingbirds of Philadelphia, Pennsylvania, singing 'Christian Automobile" or "That was Julius Cheeks and the Sensational Nightingales of Philadelphia." The Dixie Hummingbirds were initially from Greenville, South Carolina. And, though the Nightingales formed in Philadelphia, Julius Cheeks, who led them to notoriety in the 1950s, was from Spartanburg, South Carolina. They later relocated to Durham, North Carolina, the hometown of their manager, chief spokesperson, and guitarist, Jo Jo Wallace.

The smooth voice continued: "Right now, it's Reverend Claude Jeter and the Swan Silvertones of Pittsburgh, Pennsylvania, singing, 'O Mary, Don't You Weep.'" "You just heard Reverend Ruben Willingham, Little Johnny Jones and the Swanee Quintet of Augusta, Georgia, doing 'If Jesus Had to Pray, O What About Me." As he went on, the atmosphere in our little farmhouse was vibrantly charged with the sweet, clear, and soulful sound of Sam Cooke and The Soul Stirrers of Chicago, Brother Joe May, "the thunderbolt out the Midwest," The Caravans of Chicago, the Harmonizing Four of Richmond, Virginia, Clara Ward and the Ward Singers of Philadelphia, Mahalia Jackson of New Orleans, Archie Brownlee and the Five Blind Boys of Mississippi, Clarence Fountain and the Five Blind Boys of Alabama, Bob Washington and the Gospelaires of Dayton, Ohio, Joe Ligon and the Mighty Clouds of Joy of Los Angeles, and others.

Hunter was still fairly young when he died from a freak accident while working under his car. Still, memories of his impressive radio work birthed my desire to become a radio announcer. During my formative years in the Slashes Lowlands, Joe Louis Hunters' radio voice and my mother teaching me my first song helped steer me toward the fulfillment of my dreams. Yet, I could not have imagined that my first steady radio work would be co-hosting with one of the leading gospel recording artists of all time! I will share more about in Chapter Nine.

'Flintstone' Station Wagon

Four months and five days after I was born, the Supreme Court handed down the *Brown V. Board of Education* of *Topeka, Kansas*, decision, rendering school segregation unconstitutional. That landmark ruling reversed the decision the high court had rendered 58 years earlier in Plessy V. Ferguson, which sanctioned segregation. Although my parents were thrilled that the nation was moving toward racial equality, it would be many years before enforcement of the decision would even be attempted in our part of the South.

My mental development was also affected by the fact that, despite owning our land, we were dirt poor. Although many people with a similar story have said, *"we didn't know how poor we were, because everyone in the neighborhood was poor,"* we were not ignorant of our situation. Though Charlie and Gullie Reynolds had a television, and Matilda Gregory and her son, Casper, lived in a neatly painted two-story colonial house with running water and an outside spigot, we knew we and pretty much everyone else in the Slashes Lowlands were dirt poor. One way we knew was that from time to time, white people and some less impoverished black people came to our old farmhouse in trucks or cars much nicer than my father's partially wooden station wagon. Years later, when we got our first television and became familiar with the cartoon show "The Flintstones," we compared that car to the one they drove, which had no floor.

Because of holes in its worn-out floor of our car, items occasionally fell onto the road while Daddy was driving. Sometimes, Mama would ask about a certain grocery item he had gone to the store to purchase. He would reply, "I had it when I left the store." Though it was coming apart at the seams, the old jalopy passed through well-to-do white neighborhoods and took us to the nearby townships. The glaring difference in our houses was so astounding that it was impossible not to know we were poor.

The Cat in the Well

The backyard well was beneath a wooden housing structure that had a crossbeam and a pulley with a rope to let down a pail to draw water. One day, when I was about five years old, mama went to the well and was stunned to see our lifeless cat floating on top of the water. The poor feline had climbed on the well housing and lost her footing. She might have been looking down into the water and was either captivated by her own reflection or thought she saw another cat. As sad as we were by our cat's demise, we were more distressed about losing our only source of water.

Several times each day, we drew water, poured it into an aluminum pail, and placed it beside the large dish basin that functioned as our kitchen sink. But, after it was contaminated, we hauled water from the fishpond in the woods on a mule-drawn wagon and boiled it or got it from our neighbor, Ms. Matilda.

'I Got Shoes,' but only on Sundays

Poverty impacted nearly every area of our lives. Not only was there no indoor or outdoor plumbing, but my mother also prepared our meals on a stovetop and oven that had a compartment we dropped wood into and ignited. Again, kerosene lamps provided light at night, and the inside of their glass chimneys frequently darkened with soot and had to be cleaned.

Our apparel, recreation, and diet were also dictated by poverty. During the summer, we wore secondhand shoes from the "New York Bargain Store" in downtown Enfield only on Sundays. Wearing shoes just one day a week extended their use until school started in the fall. You could find inexpensive clothing and shoes at this second-hand store. You also got exactly what you paid for. You spent little and got next to worthless merchandise.

I can still feel the warm soil and smooth blades of grass under my feet as we made our way to and from the fields each day or played baseball on a hot Saturday evening in the front yard, swinging makeshift bats made from tree limbs. Almost all our toys were homemade. We made bows and arrows, slingshots, kites, and wooden bull bellows. For snacks or to supplement meals, in the winter, we climbed into the barn loft and picked peanuts from bales of peanut hay, roasted them in our wood-burning oven, and sometimes made peanut brittle for dessert. When it snowed, we made snow ice cream, a truly special treat! Though we had little, we used what we had effectively.

"I Don' Killed Myself!"

Growing up, my brother Griffin and I often found ourselves in precarious situations. One day, we were picking peanuts in the hayloft. To reach them, we had to climb a rickety wooden ladder that led straight up to a two-by-two-foot opening in the floor of the loft. The ladder's design was simple but treacherous - two vertical beams with horizontal steps made of two-by-fours that jutted out on either side. The edges of those steps were more dangerous than we knew.

As we worked in the loft, Griffin accidentally stepped too close to the opening and lost his footing. As he fell, he tumbled through the hole, striking his head on the protruding ladder steps near the bottom. The impact made a deep gash in his left temple, and blood began flowing profusely. Panicked and disoriented, the seven-year-old became convinced he was dying. He ran from the barn towards our house, shouting hysterically, "I've killed myself! I'm dead! I know I'm dead!" Hearing the commotion, our parents quickly assessed the situation. They bundled Griffin into the car and rushed him to Dr. White's office in nearby Halifax.

Dr. White had a great bedside manner. He would claim to have experienced every condition anyone brought to him. So, he calmly shared with Griffin about the time he had fallen from a hayloft and knocked a hole in his temple. Listening to him, Griffin no longer believed he was dead and suddenly had hope that he would live! He survived with only a scar from the stitches.

This incident served to remind me of the hidden dangers that can lurk in the most familiar places and how quickly a routine chore can turn into a frightening emergency. And that little scar reminds me that, like Dr. White, who always seemed to know what to say to his patients to change their gloomy outlook, I always have hope. The angels watching over me can always transform any dismal circumstances and lead me to the light! Lessons I learned in Sunday School, such as when Uncle F confronted a serpent in church or gleaned from the bedside manner of a small-town doctor, assure me of continuous hope.

King David confidently declared, **"All day long,** I *put my hope in you" (Ps 25:5 NLT).* No part of the day is left for despairing! Even if, like Griffin, I feel hopeless, I have hope for it because "all night, all day, the angels are watching over me!"

Flight of Terror!

Betty and I had a harrowing experience during a trip to Kenya. One morning, we left our hotel in Nairobi and headed to Jomo Kenyatta Airport to connect with a team of seven fellow mission workers for a flight to Kisumu. From there, we would be driven via a small van for several hours over rough and bumpy roads to Kakamega to begin a medical, educational, and spiritual mission. Unfortunately, the team arrived late at the airport, and we missed our flight. So, our leader decided that we would go to the smaller Wilson Airport to charter a plane for the trip.

We arrived at the airport and began negotiations for the charter flight, for which all of us were asked to help pay. *This did not sit well with Betty since we had been on time for the scheduled flight, but she held her peace.* After a couple of hours of negotiations, a small plane, one that had clearly seen many years of flying was secured. An old retired Kenyan Air Force pilot who had been aroused from a deep sleep and, unbeknownst to us, had imbibed alcohol for breakfast was talked into flying the plane.

Since the plane's capacity was twelve passengers and there were nine people on our mission team, we *should* have been fine. Betty and I were traveling light with one medium-sized suitcase each. However, most team members had several oversized pieces of luggage that exceeded the plane's cargo space capacity. So, the one-man flight attendant crew packed suitcases in seats and the aisle as I squinted in disbelief and glanced briefly at Betty, who looked stunned. The little plane was so jammed it looked like a 1950s fad in which twenty-five or more people crammed into a phone booth or a Volkswagen Beetle.

When we began to detect the smell of alcohol on our pilot's breath, I began thinking perhaps this was a secret taping of the Candid Camera television show—except it had stopped production years earlier. I do not know why no one protested or simply said, "This is unsafe." It might be that, at the moment, we were paralyzed and too shocked to think clearly.

After a moment of prayer, the plane began taxiing down the runway. As it struggled to become airborne, the strain on the engine was so strong it felt as though we would go down at any moment! There was an eerie, deafening silence on board, and no one uttered a word throughout the flight. Still, everyone's lips were moving. Team members gripped their seat handles, quietly praying with tears trickling down their cheeks. A look of utter terror was on everyone's face! We landed safely in Kisumu about an hour later, and after the luggage was unloaded from the aisle and we deplaned, robust sighs of relief and exhilarating shouts of "Thank you, Jesus!" replaced the silence.

Now this is the part that I am hesitant to share as storytellers are expected to be the butt of their jokes rather than make themselves look good. But there is no "joke" in this story. I was probably just too dumb to appreciate the danger we faced. Or maybe I was not thinking deeply enough about it. But despite seeing the luggage crammed in the cabin, hearing the strain of the engine, and smelling the alcohol on the pilot's breath, I had an inexplicable sense of peace. Whether I saw but didn't grasp the gravity of the situation, I do not know. But the peace I felt was from the angel of the LORD who was encamped around me (Psalm 34:7). The song my mother taught me as a child, the image of Uncle F attacking the dangerous serpent, and the scriptures my father pushed me to read were working!

"And do not be anxious about anything, but in everything by prayer and supplication with thanksgiving let your requests be made know to God. And the peace of God, which surpasses all understanding, will guard your hearts and your minds in Christ Jesus" (Phil 4:5-7 ESV).

High in the air on a little overcrowded plane between Nairobi and Kisumu, Kenya, I was standing on the promises of God, filled with peace and confident **hope**!

Five
Barriers

Despite learning the need to face fears and develop confident hope, seeds of inferiority were also planted deep in my mind. Due to the complex economic system, to maintain our farm's operations, our family was compelled to borrow money from Mr. Barnwell (not his real name), a prosperous white businessman. He was a despicable character who believed in strictly enforced segregation and second-class citizenship for black people. That "loan shark" not only relished using the N-word, but ensured that we remained perpetually indebted to him for as long as we lived on land *we owned*. And we were essentially trapped in unpaid labor, akin to slavery, on our own land!

Once, when my father had gone to town for groceries, he drove onto our front yard and loudly blew his horn. As Mama stepped onto the porch to see what he wanted, he barked at her. "Tell Jesse to come out here." When Mama responded, "he's not here," The enraged man shouted back at her, "He is here! I know he's in there. Now tell that ole floppy-eared mule to come out here!"

But my mother did not accept disrespect from anyone. So, looking him straight in the eye, she calmly but firmly stated again, "He is not here," then turned, walked back inside, and closed the door. Since my father always treated everyone with kindness and respect, whether they deserved it or not, he had not given Mr. Barnwell any reason to speak to my mother so rudely.

My father told us of another incident involving Mr. Barnwell some years later, after the 1964 Civil Rights Act ended legal segregation in restaurants and other establishments. Barnwell related how a "colored man," in a restaurant in Enfield where he was having dinner, responded to the white waitress' question by saying, "Huh?" Barnwell told my father that the response made his blood boil, and "I could not believe he said "huh" to a white woman!" I wanted to bust that n----r in the face!" He believed in white supremacy and thought it was okay to speak to my father about another black man in that way. He thought the other man's response should have been "Ma'am?" to show that he understood his place. Though he had the legal right to be in the restaurant, Barnwell saw him as inferior to the white waitress. My father's only response was to step away from the conversation and quietly pray for him. To escape our lop-sided economic situation, as soon as the opportunity presented itself, we moved to Enfield and became sharecroppers on another wealthy white aristocrat's land. Although this situation was almost as confining as what we left in Halifax, at the end of the first year, the six hundred dollars my family had was considerably more than we ever earned on our own farm.

During those years, I internalized the rules and folkways of de jure and de facto segregation. A public park featuring a Confederate monument as its centerpiece was located within walking distance of my house, providing a space where white residents could go for recreation and relaxation. Though Enfield Graded School was a short walk from where we lived, I was being bussed several miles across town and over the railroad tracks to the separate and unequal T. S. Inborden School. Many of our books and other materials had been discarded after years of use at Enfield Graded. Subconsciously, seeds of low self-esteem were being planted deep inside me, and I was subtly inhaling atmospheric inferiority. I found myself in a battle to overcome the fear of being perceived as less than the privileged people who lived in nice houses, drove decent cars, and could go to parks or schools where I was forbidden.

Instruments of Fear

The hostility of the Enfield Graded School environment was not the only tool in the hands of the Spirit of fear. Sharecropping was taxing and difficult. Few things, if any, could have been more humbling than the years spent laboring in cotton, peanuts, corn, and tobacco fields in Enfield. *Priming* tobacco by breaking off the ripe, bright yellowish leaves of each stalk and piling them into mule-pulled trucks was a challenging task. Our backs were constantly bent and hurting, and we were annoyed by the presence of huge, bright green tobacco hornworms on the leaves. Black, sticky tobacco "gum" accumulated on our hands and arms. The searing heat caused sweat to drip from our foreheads into our eyes, and as we attempted to wipe it away, the gluey stuff would burn our eyes and cause them to fill with tears.

I am Dyin' O Lord!

To harvest the crop in time, we joined forces with my father's youngest brother, Howard Henry Sumner, Sr., and his family each season, trading off weeks in each other's fields. While struggling in the scorching heat, my cousin, Walter, could at times be heard singing mournfully his own rendition of the old Fanny Crosby hymn, **"Draw Me Nearer."**

*I am **Dyin'** O Lord.*
I have heard thy voice.
And it told thy love to me.
And be closer drawn to Thee.

Walter changed the actual first line from "*I am* **thine**," to "*I am dyin*" to cunningly capture our feelings and make us chuckle as we endured the miserable task. He inherited his wit through generations of ancestors who had provided forced labor, including our great-great grandfather Philo Sumner.

The Negro spirituals they composed were packed with coded language only they understood. Songs such as *"Sinner, Please, Don't Let this Harvest Pass"* had hidden meanings. The composer of these lyrics sought to convey that his fellow slaves might lose their lives by holding such militant gatherings, but otherwise, they might lose their souls."

> *Sinner, please don't let this harvest pass. Sinner, please don't let this harvest pass. Sinner, please don't let this harvest pass, And die and lose your soul at last.*

In his 1937 classic treatiste on southern social culture, *Caste and Class in a Southern Town*, John Dollard vividly exposed the Southern antebellum caste system that sharecropping represented. The system, which remained prominent until the 1960s, was steeped in entrenched racist ideology. Though Southern black people endured its harshest form, variants existed in the other regions of the country.

Our landowner in Enfield had a slave master's mentality. Occasionally, he and his family would ride through the fields on horseback as we picked cotton. While our bodies were bent into 45-degree angles and we filled sacks strapped to our shoulders with cotton from sharp-pointed bowls of cotton, we peered at them from the corners of our eyes. Although the landowner could not recapture what Margaret Mitchell called a civilization that was "*gone with the wind,*" he succeeded in making us feel enslaved on our own property. His optics conveyed the message that we were trapped in the 'peculiar' restraining institution with no escape to which historian Kenneth M. Stampp referred. Though we had voluntarily entered sharecropping to free ourselves from the enslaving economic system of Halifax, an equally oppressive system encircled us with an invisible but imposing barrier that prevented movement or access.

Barriers attempt to lock us in or out and block our forward progress. As Bishop Alfred Owens, Jr. stated in a sermon entitled, "Stop Being Scared: Scarecrows," "They are set up to provoke fear. But these are scarecrows that cannot cause real harm. And a scarecrow is never set up in an unprofitable field." Sometimes, barriers suddenly appear in the road with no apparent way to get over, around, or through them. At other times, they are **seemingly** impenetrable blockades like gates of brass or bars of iron appearing as impossible odds, physical weariness, mental stress, or self-doubt.

There were many days on that farm when I felt barricaded inside a dead-end system. Those barriers subconsciously affected my thinking about my capacity to accomplish great things. Despite my claims of knowing and loving the majestic God, walking in his royal light, and serving as a soldier in his army, I found myself sinking further into a mindset plagued by fear, crushed dreams, and deadly thoughts. This descent was fueled not only by racist intimidation and but also by self-imposed limitations and **barriers.**

Mom and Dad

My sisters, Denise and Venise, Daddy's 1958 Pontiac Chieftain and the front porch of our old farmhouse

Howard Sumner, FG Sumner, Jesse Sumner, Sr.

Gospel radio announcing on WDUR AM/WFXC FM

Singing with Evangelist Mae Newton and the Mathis Singers on the Bobby Jones's Gospel Show

Greeting students in the lobby of North Bethesda Middle School

Addressing student assembly at North Bethesda Middle School

Six
Daddy

"See how very much our Father loves us, for he calls us his children, and that is what we are!"
1 Jn. 3:1a NLT

My dad's years of grueling labor took a heavy toll, wearing him down and eventually leading to a seven-month hospitalization with a serious spinal condition. Though we were all drained, his encouraging words about the divine vision God had given him for his children continued to resonate deeply within us and drive us onward and upward.

"Enough Fools"

Daddy stopped the car in front of Mutt Well's Little Country Store off Highway 481 at the western edge of Enfield, which was our favorite place to buy snacks. The proprietor was a middle-aged white man with a kind, friendly disposition. Black and white men often congregated in his store to "shoot the breeze," crack jokes, and blow off steam.

Once, when I was about fourteen, I stayed in the car while Daddy went in to get snacks since he would be returning quickly. When he returned to the car, he glanced over while starting the engine and dropped a bit of wisdom on me. I was accustomed to these frequent nuggets because he never stopped teaching us to navigate the challenges of life. But what he said at that moment caught me by surprise and would echo within me for the rest of my life. *"Son, always remember. There're enough fools in the world already. You don't need to be one."* While it had never been my plan to add to the population of fools, after hearing this, I became more resolute than ever to make wise life decisions! I knew my father was not knocking me. He was pulling for me. He was on my side and wanted me to be successful in life.

When Dr. Maya Angelou was once asked if children can learn resilience on their own, she stressed the importance of young people having someone there for them. *"If we have someone who loves us—I don't mean who indulges us, but who loves us enough to be on our side—then it's easier to grow resilience, to grow belief in self, to grow self-esteem. And its self-esteem that allows a person to stand up."*

Like children, our capacity to quickly and fully recover after being knocked down is connected with who is with us, pulling for us, and caring for us.

"I will be a Father to You, and you shall be My sons and daughters, says the LORD Almighty." 2 Cor 6:18 NKJV.

When we are attacked by circumstances, we must remember that the LORD Almighty is our Father. He is not a distant relative who doesn't really care about us. **He is our Father, our heavenly Father, who is intimately concerned about us!**

Though his formal schooling ended in the fifth grade, my father was a wise man. The wisdom he unsparingly shared with my siblings and me had been acquired in the "University of Life," often called the University of Hard Knocks. Although farm life was hard, he was determined not to allow it to deny us a secure shot at formal education as it had done him.

Meta Tauta! (After This!)

"After this I looked, and behold, a door was opened in heaven" (Rev 4:1).

Daddy was born one year after the Tulsa Massacre and the burning of Black Wall Street. Two years later, the Rosewood Massacre in Levy County, Florida, annihilated the citizens of another predominantly African American community. He garnered much experience from years of shaking peanuts. This task involved grasping the foot-long, leafy green vines of freshly plowed peanut plants and shaking mud from the large clusters attached to their roots. Afterward, the vines and peanuts were stacked onto haystack poles throughout the fields.

Before this could be done, Daddy, Jesse Jr., Griffin, and I loaded mule-pulled wagons and headed into the woods to identify and chop down suitable trees to make haystack poles. Returning to the field, we used post hole diggers to excavate evenly spaced holes for each pole, and after firmly securing and stabilizing them in their hole, we fashioned two slats into a t-shape at the bottom of each pole, out of leftover wood cuttings. What was mere tedium for us taught him organizational skills, precision, and patience.

Daddy also used the wisdom gleaned from years of slopping pigs, feeding, and watering mules, horses, cows, and chickens to formulate a vision for our future. While we toiled in the fields under the scorching afternoon sun, he persistently reassured us that our challenging circumstances were only temporary. He promised us that just as the seeds we planted in the ground underfoot soon emerged and flourished, so would we. He urged us to persevere through high school and pursue higher education despite the significant challenges we faced. With eyes of faith within the depths of his being, like John's divine revelations on the island of Patmos, he experienced a profound spiritual awakening that transcended our immediate circumstances. In the Book of Revelation, the Apostle used the Greek term "meta tauta" to preface his vision of an open door in heaven.

While we were languishing behind the barriers of a burdensome sharecropping system and a racist society, Daddy held on to a heavenly vision of an open door through which we would someday walk and repeatedly told us that something much greater was coming for us—meta tauta! "This too will pass," he regularly reminded us. "One day, you will be looking back on what we are going through," he would say.

But this was not without cost. Our responsibility was to **pray, prepare, persevere, pursue** education, and stand on the promises of our heavenly Father! Like Horace Mann, the father of public-school education, who said, *"[e]ducation... beyond all other devices of human origin, is the great equalizer of the conditions of men,"* my parents believed that their children's **pursuit of** education was an essential part of securing a successful future. Their strong faith was based on their consistent, effectual, fervent conversation with God, their *perfect love* for Him, and their *love* for their children. They modeled *"Pray without ceasing" (1 Thess 5:17 KJV)*, all the while putting work behind their prayers.

Clearly, my father's perfect love for us led him to assure us unceasingly that if we continued our education, *one day* we *would* be able to stand shoulder to shoulder with anyone and look them in the eye, regardless of their race.

Guarding the Vision

"Be sober, be vigilant; because your adversary the devil walks about like a roaring lion, seeking whom he may devour." 1 Peter 5:8 NKJV

Visions and dreams, like vegetables and other crops, need to be carefully guarded to prevent them from being stolen or destroyed. So, Daddy safeguarded his vision for our future from potential enemies.

Everyone in the neighborhood knew that alcohol was never brought into our home. Yet once, when Mom and Dad had gone to town on an errand, Bud McGee and one of his buddies showed up at our back door with cans of beer and asked for an opener. While my siblings and I looked at the men and saw beer cans up close for the first time, Dad returned home and walked to the back door. When he saw what was happening, he became enraged and shouted to the men: *"Get away from my children! You know who I am, and what I stand for. You are up to no good, drinking alcohol in front of them and asking for a can opener! Don't ever let me catch you coming around here with that stuff again!"* They hurried off to the footpath leading into the woods.

In one Sunday school lesson, I learned how Jesus became enraged at the merchants plying their trade in the temple in Jerusalem—His Father's house, the house of prayer, and angrily drove them out. My daddy's house, like that temple, was a house of prayer and biblical teaching. Like Jesus, Daddy saw Bud and his friend as 'thieves' who were attempting to rob his children of our innocence and distract us from his teaching about good and evil. And like the serpent in the garden, they could be trying to persuade us to accept as good what our father had taught us was forbidden. To remain on course and complete our education, we would have to be sober and vigilant. My father saw anyone who tempted us to drink alcohol as an adversary prowling like a roaring lion and seeking someone to devour. Ultimately, all eight siblings completed college.

Undoubtable Faith

I learned and garnered even more from observing Daddy every day. Without always verbalizing everything, he taught me that each of us has the capacity to accomplish far more. He read everything of value he could get his hands on—books, magazines, and newspapers. And, of course, he read *the Bible* and also challenged me to read it. At first, I was annoyed by his frequent insistence and found much of it difficult to comprehend. But as time has passed, regular Scripture reading has become imperative, and I comprehend it more clearly.

One passage in particular—John 21:25—convinced me that I can do much more than I have done. In that verse, Jesus had done so much in a short span that the Apostle could not tell it all in his Gospel. His book begins with Jesus working at God's side "In the beginning" (John 1:1 KJV) during Creation. He then takes us to Jesus' baptism and the start of his ministry at 30 years of age and shares Jesus' life-changing conversation with a member of Israel's supreme court. which includes the central message of the Bible, "For God so loved the world that He gave his only begotten son, that whosoever believeth in him should not perish, but have everlasting life" (John 3:16 KJV). He guides his readers through the Crucifixion and Resurrection and concludes that if everything Jesus did were written, the world would not contain the volume of books required. And John quotes Jesus saying,

> *"Anyone who believes in me will do the same works I have done, and even greater works"* (John 14:12 NLT).

Jesus accomplished those things by faith! Every believer has a measure of this same God-given faith. Yet, we also have a measure of doubt given to us by God's enemy—the devil! Consequently, our faith is, too often, tempered with doubt.

In the Gospel of Mark, a father brought his son to Jesus to be healed, but wanted Jesus to know just how difficult it was likely to be.

"He is possessed by an evil spirit that won't let him talk," he explained. *And whenever this spirit seizes him, it throws him violently to the ground. Then he foams at the mouth and grinds his teeth and becomes rigid."*

He went on to tell Jesus that,

"I asked your disciples to cast out the evil spirit, but they couldn't do it."

The father added,

"The spirit often throws him into the fire or into the water, trying to kill him."

Then, with a desperate plea, he begged,

"Have mercy on us and help us, if you can." When Jesus responded, that *"anything is possible if you believe,"*

The father replied,

"I do believe," but added tearfully, *"but help me overcome my unbelief (Mk 9:17-24 NLT)*

Faith is neutralized and rendered ineffective when we counterbalance it with uncertainty. So, like that father, we need help with our unbelief. We must ask God to help us not to doubt and then ensure that what we ask God for is according to *His will*.

I have developed the basics of doubtless (undoubtable) faith—the BDF Principle. In Matthew 21, the disciples were amazed at how quickly the fig tree withered after Jesus commanded it never to bear fruit again. He told them that they had the same power if they had faith and did not doubt!

So, we rise to the level of un*doubtable faith by* simply applying the BDF principle. In school, we were taught the three "R's," reading, writing, and arithmetic as the basics of learning. The basics of doubtless faith are four "R's." Remember, recognize, request, return!

Remember who said it. There is no more authoritative source than Jesus, the incarnate God. He is the one who said,

"If you have faith and do not doubt..."
(Matt 21:21)

Recognize your unbelief and, like the father in Mark, be honest and acknowledge your problem.

Request help with your doubts. Jesus did not condemn the father for his honest request. "Help me overcome my unbelief" (Mk 9:24).

Return doubt to the devil! Give it back to the one who sold it to you! As believers, we are admonished to take back what the devil stole from us. But before you can **take** back what he *stole* from you, you must **give** back what he *sold* to you!

By applying the uncomplicated but powerful BDF principle, you can have *doubtless faith* and can get what you want from God so long as it is according to His will. The devil said, *"You can't!"* But Jesus said, *"**You can!**"* Whose report will you believe?

Practicing the BDF principle: *Remember, recognize, request,* and *return* will help you have faith without wavering! You *can* go back to school and get that degree! You *can* be healed and get well again! You *can* catch that dream you've been chasing! You *can* reach your goal! You *can* fulfill your mission!

The F.A.I.T.H. of My Father

Daddy never lost focus on what was important because he saw faith as a verb—an action word! For him, faith was not merely believing and trusting but it was made visible by doing something! In one account in the book of Mark, four men dropped their paralytic friend through the roof of a house to get him to Jesus, and Jesus *saw* their faith (Mk 2:3-5). In another instance, a woman with an issue of blood made her faith visible by touching the fringe of Jesus' robe. When he saw who had touched his clothes, he said to her, *"Daughter, your faith has healed you. Go in peace and be freed from your suffering"* (Mk 5:34 NIV). So, faith is not an abstract concept. Rather, it involves concrete action. During my time as a secondary school principal, a friend and co-worker devised an acrostic for faith that fits my father well. Dr. Bell asked me, "How do you spell faith?" I responded, F-A-I-T-H. He said, "Let's look at each letter in faith to define what it is. "**F**inding **A**nswers **I**n **t**he **H**and! **F**inding **A**nswers **I**n **T**he **H**ead! **F**inding **A**nswers **I**n **T**he **H**eart! **F**inding **A**nswers **I**n **T**he **H**ell!"

Finding **A**nswers **I**n **T**he **H**and! My father always worked to help anyone in need in any way he could. He visited the sick and those in nursing homes, fed the hungry, mowed the church grass, painted and paneled the walls, and so much more!

Finding **A**nswers **I**n **T**he **H**ead! His mind was never idle. He read and studied incessantly. I saw him at all hours of the night studying and preparing sermons.

Finding **A**nswers **I**n the **H**eart! He loved his family deeply and did everything he could for us. He loved the church and had the true heart of a genuine pastor.

Finding **A**nswers **I**n the **H**ell!" When he was in the hospital for seven months and paralyzed for eight weeks, my father used that time to study scriptures, pray, and develop a more excellent ministry. When our pastor resigned less than two years later, and the pastorate fell upon him, though some members left, the church began to grow.

The last two sermons I heard my father preach are indelibly etched in my brain. In one entitled, *"If You Know These Things, Happy are Ye, if You Do Them,"* he *spoke of what* Jesus said to his disciples after washing their feet following the Last Supper. He admonished them to serve God and his people with humility. The final sermon, *"Young Man, Stand Upon Thy Feet!"* taken from Ezekiel 2:1, spoke of when the prophet was called by God after he had a vision by the Chebar River. Through the words of the passage, *"Son of Man, stand upon thy feet, and I will speak unto thee,"* By way of Ezekiel 2:1, God was letting me know that, at Age 21, he was speaking to me. Three days before God called him home, as I was getting into the car to drive back to Durham, my father followed me out of the house and admonished me to maintain my faith in God and always do what is right. I know now that God was speaking to me through a man who was a true reflection of himself—**Daddy**.

Seven
Resilience

When adversity surrounds you, and it seems as if the hounds of hell have been turned loose, you desperately need answers! And you need resilient, active faith to lift you out of such dire circumstances and propel you forward. No matter how difficult things became, Daddy never lost his vision for his family or church.

"When the Dog Bites"

It happened on a beautiful summer Saturday morning when I was about 13 years old. Puffs of white clouds dotted the blue sky, and gentle breezes trickled through the leaves of the trees. Since our Enfield farm was at the edge of the city limits on the white side of town, Mama would occasionally send me on the two-mile walk to Meyers' Grocery store in town to get something needed to prepare dinner. I was happy to go because I might be allowed to purchase a treat such as a Zero candy bar, a small pack of caramel Sugar Babies, a Baby Ruth candy bar, or perhaps a bag of Vanilla Wafers.

This scenic walk took me past lush green fields on either side of a long dirt path leading to McFarland Road where I would turn right. Strolling across the intersecting Franklin Street, I passed the white-only cemetery and park. Eventually, coming to Main Street, I turned left and continued past the charming Victorian and Colonial homes of the white people. Mama always reminded me to be alert and stay focused until I returned home.

After making my purchase, I headed back down Main Street. As I walked, KC, a white girl whose dad owned the local drugstore where I sometimes stopped to purchase ice cream, came toward me on the sidewalk, accompanied by her large, spotted Dalmatian. At the time, Enfield had no leash law, and the dog slyly moved back behind her, presumably I thought, so I could pass her without having to step into the grass. The rather attractive girl seemed friendly enough.

As we crossed paths, KC offered a subtle smile and a brief "Hi." So, as I glanced in her direction and returned the greeting. Suddenly, I felt a searing pain in my left thigh. Without warning, the dog viciously attacked me, its sharp teeth tearing into my flesh! I stood there in shock, blood soaking through my pants, struggling to comprehend the sudden turn of events. Why did the dog bite me? Did it bite everyone who returned a greeting to its owner? My head was spinning but the blood dripping down my leg forced me to run home quickly.

I had been oblivious to the danger I faced when I saw KC approaching. Little did I know that even a glance or a word exchanged with her was akin to tasting forbidden fruit. It was only a fleeting moment. However, this brief lapse in attention, in which I ignored my mother's advice to stay alert and focused, resulted in an injury that left me bleeding and in need of a tetanus shot.

If Adam and Eve had remained focused on God's instructions in the Garden of Eden, and if Eve had not been captivated by the tree's beauty and the allure of its fruit, she might have realized she was taking advice from a serpent.

Suppose I had maintained my focus and not been momentarily distracted by a pretty face and smile, I might have noticed that the seemingly innocent girl was part of a package of forbidden fruit and that a vicious animal had quietly positioned itself behind her, ready to strike. My injury resulted from disregarding my mother's advice to stay alert and focused. By losing sight of the broader situation, I failed to notice that the dog had quietly gone into attack mode.

Prior to this incident, I had never been afraid of dogs. However, in the aftermath, it took a considerable amount of time before I could overcome my fear of certain breeds, particularly large Dalmatians. Ultimately, though, this experience imparted a valuable lesson about the importance of maintaining focus on the bigger picture and being mindful of potentially costly and painful distractions.

"No Bird Soars in a Calm."

David McCullough's compelling book, *The Wright Brothers*, provides an account of Wilbur and Orville Wright's challenging attempt to build a heavier-than-air machine to enable humans to fly. I was fascinated by how much time they spent studying and observing birds. The story begins with a childhood gift from their father that sparked their interest in flight and concluded with their posthumously honored by Neil Armstrong during the Gemini 8 mission to the moon.

The book highlights the crucial role that the brothers' extensive study and observation of birds played in their understanding of flight mechanics. Despite having only a high school education, limited financial resources, and no influential connections, the pair remained undeterred in their mission, and their unwavering focus allowed them to overcome seemingly insurmountable challenges.

The narrative of their often painful struggle details primarily how two family members—their father, Bishop Milton Wright, and their younger sister Katharine, who nursed Orville back to health when a trial flight crashed and nearly took his life—figure prominently in the saga. The themes of resilience and unyielding resolve loom large as the brothers confront mounting obstacles and setbacks. Though they encountered severe turbulence, they never buckled under the pressure but were determined to see the mission through. Distractions like the birth of the automobile industry momentarily took Wilbur's attention away from the mission. But as he would later proclaim, **"No bird soars in a calm."**

The brothers never showed vengeance or greed and were content to live modestly, though they endured countless failures, including the crash of the trial flight. And while today, we cannot imagine life without air travel, it is inspiring to see how it developed from an idea in the minds of two little boys whose father gave them a tiny flying toy.

Though they faced criticism and opposition, the brothers ultimately remained committed to their vision. The only response they wished to offer their critics was their success. Despite the fact that the Wrights were a white, middle- class family living comfortable mid-western lives, while my impoverished black family struggled to survive the Southern sharecropping system, the book resonated strongly with me, for there were some similarities. My father, like Bishop Wright, was a minister. He gave us the gift of his love for learning. He read to us, instructed us, and shared his vision of a better future for us. Though Wilbur was briefly distracted from his mission, he quickly regained his focus and rejoined his brother in pursuing their true objective. My father faced numerous adversaries who wished to see him fail, yet he remained steadfast in his mission. He protected us from major distractions.

In the 1950s, as television sets began to appear in American homes on a widespread basis, the fascination was so great that even some poor families we knew purchased one. But owning a television was not a priority for my parents. Since we loved reading and saw it as essential for learning, they felt that a television set would be a distraction. Developing creative imagination was also critical for us. Our entertainment was a console radio, and listening to radio broadcasts required more imagination than watching television since we could only hear the action.

The Silver Trumpet

While most of our toys were homemade, I will always remember a gift from my father. One Christmas, Daddy woke me up at about 2:00 a.m. to give me a toy he had purchased for me. Mama watched, smiling, as Daddy could not wait until daybreak to give me a little silver trumpet from the Roses Five and Ten store. Though I was only about three years old, I have never forgotten that simple act of love, and that special moment and that special moment when my daddy woke me in the middle of the night to give me a gift will always be sky high among my fondest memories! Wow! Even as I write this, the image of my father shaking me awake in the middle of the night to give me that special Christmas gift causes warm tears to form in my eyes.

I have only recently understood the connection between that trumpet and my broader life purpose. In the Bible, the trumpet was associated with *movement* and *victory*. Each of Gideon's 300 men had a *trumpet*. (Judg 7:16). The fall of the walls of Jericho followed a long blast on *trumpets* (Josh 6:20). Two silver *trumpets* called the community of Israel together to set out on their sojourn in the wilderness (Num 10:2). Isaiah was told to lift his voice like a *trumpet* to warn the people of Israel (Is 58:1).

I have always been told that my speaking voice is a gift from God, so my voice must be used to sound out the victorious message of the Gospel. In the second grade, I played a game in which we had to disguise our voices to see if a blindfolded student could identify us. When I disguised my voice, the blindfolded student said, "Alton, there is no way anybody is not going to know your voice!" In eighth grade, I did a report on Bolivia. Though other students used colorful graphics as props, I did my report without graphics. My teacher gave me an "A" and remarked, "You have such a wonderful speaking voice! Very pleasant to listen to." In the early 1970s, theologian Dr. James Forbes, Jr., asked me, "Has the Lord spoken to you about your voice yet?"

For over 13 years, I served as a radio announcer for a top-rated Sunday morning inspirational show. Later,

I became an ordained minister. Through these years, I have often reflected on the cherished memory of the inexpensive toy my father gave me in the middle of the night when I was three years old. It was all he could afford, and though it only lasted until mid-afternoon on Christmas Day, its value and meaning have endured <u>to this day</u>.

Daddy's resilience and ability to rebound from the hard blows he sustained were also not lost to me. I would have to repeatedly bounce back from numerous blows. Besides the threats and lies following that junior high fight and being assigned to a lower-level academic group despite having higher test scores than the majority of the white class, I had to develop the tenacity to survive that toxic environment. Students made racist comments to me and the other three African American students. They would say things like, *"I heard that n----r's brains were in their toes."* Or remark, *"Must be gonna rain today. All these black clouds floating around in here.* Or, *"N----r, you better skip two seats between us when we go into the auditorium."* To endure the challenging desegregation experiment and the belittling, pseudo-slavery conditions of sharecropping, I had to *grow* **resilience**.

Eight
Mama

"I cried out, 'I am slipping!' but your unfailing love, O LORD, supported me. When doubts filled my mind, your comfort gave me renewed hope and cheer."

Ps 94:18-19 NLT

Mama was *a reflection of God's true love. She was* born in 1924, the third of four children of Mason and Esther Floyd Davis. When she was little more than a toddler, her mother died, so she did not remember her but relied on the memories of her older siblings. Her sister, Beatrice, was eight, and her brother, Marion, was six at the time of their mother's death. She and her younger brother, Floyd, who was barely two at the time, were raised by their maternal grandmother, Alice Floyd, whom they called Granny. Beatrice and Buddy stayed with their father since they were older and could do more for themselves.

Granny was sixty years old when she took Mama and Uncle Floyd into her home. She was a former school teacher with high hopes for Lillie Belle, who had a strong thirst for knowledge during her years as a student at Shady Grove Elementary School. In those days, black children had to take a high school entrance examination to gain acceptance. And they could only take the exam if their seventh-grade teacher recommended them. Mama was one of ten students recommended from her seventh-grade class. And only three of them passed the exam and were accepted into Enfield's Brick High School.

Mama loved high school, especially English and drama classes taught by her favorite teacher, Miss Gladys Hammond. But there are always obstacles and opposition wherever there are opportunities. So, at one point early on during her time at the school, the only way to get to the school bus was to pass through the yard of a white woman who had vicious dogs. The dogs would try to prevent Mama from crossing the yard. So, she regularly would have to defend herself with whatever was in her hand and run from them. Since the woman told Mama she did not want her to cross her yard, Granny contacted her cousin, Minnie Bobbitt, who lived closer to where the bus stopped, and Minnie allowed Mama to live with her until the unfriendly woman and her dogs moved away.

Mama excelled in school and loved poetry by classic writers like Emily Dickinson and James Weldon Johnson. She was college-bound and on course to enter a professional career. Granny probably expected her to enroll at her alma mater, historic Shaw University, the first historically black university in the South. But the trajectory of my mother's life would change within a short time.

In 1941, on the last day of school, Lillie Belle spotted her classmate, Carrie Viola Sumner, standing across the campus with a tall, handsome gentleman. Seeing Lillie Belle, Carrie turned to the gentleman and said rather excitedly, "There she is!" Calling Mama over, she made the introduction. "Lillie Belle, this is my brother, Jesse. Jesse, this is the girl I've been telling you about, Lillie Belle Davis," then turned and disappeared, like Cupid taking flight after shooting his arrow of love. She left the two standing there, not sure what to say to each other. But Cupid's arrow had struck its target dead center!

The attraction was immediate, and Lillie Belle eventually invited Jesse Eugene Sumner to a July 4th program she was coordinating. Jesse attended, and the flame was kindled. In 1942, when Jesse was 22 and Lillie Belle was 18, the 6-foot, 3-inch *farm* boy, who dropped out of school after the fifth grade, and the attractive college-bound high school graduate fell in love and began to speak of marriage.

Although by 1939, the Great Depression had essentially ended for white Americans, most black Americans were still feeling its full effects. Three years later, Granny knew that if Lillie Belle and Jesse married, her hopes of seeing her granddaughter go to college and securing a professional career would likely be replaced by tedious farm life.

At first, Alice Floyd, a rare black professional woman, might surely have protested vehemently and insisted that Lille Belle not abandon her career plans to marry a poor, uneducated farmer. But Granny was also a wise, God-fearing woman who saw something in Jesse that assured her she would not have to worry about her granddaughter's future. She affirmed that Jesse was a man of great character, and she would be happy for Lillie Belle to marry him. If Granny had a different mindset, or if Lillie Belle had not accepted Jesse's proposal, I would never have been born!

By 1965, 45-year-old Jesse Sr. and 41-year-old Lillie Belle were parents of eight children. The family had survived the Slashes Lowlands and was sharecropping in Enfield. Though each of us helped keep the farm going, late that summer, Jesse Sr. became desperately ill with a spinal condition. This was a time when the tobacco and corn stalks were growing tall, the cotton plants were displaying their fuchsia and white blossoms and would soon put out bolls of fluffy white cotton. The peanuts fields were covered with sprawling green peanut vines and yellow blooms.

When he was hospitalized in early September, we did not know that it would be seven months before Daddy was discharged. Even then, for three additional months, he was wrapped in a waist-to-his-chin body cast and had to sleep on a hospital bed at home. Jesse Jr. had been drafted into the army a year earlier. Helena and Louetta were attending college in Durham. Seeing them complete college was a major part of my parents' dream. Now, Mama struggled to manage the farm and care for the five children still at home. I was eleven, Gwen and Griffin were in their early teens, and the twins were only four years old and had not begun to attend school.

One evening, Griffin and I were racing bareback on two mules in the back pasture as we often did for recreation after a hard day's work in the fields. There was nothing like the feel of the wind on our faces as the mules broke into a fast, steady gallop! And this was our way of escaping the dire realities of sharecropping and feeling free for an hour! Suddenly, Griffin's high-spirited, conniving beast took him too close to a ground wire, brushed his leg against it, and threw him, breaking his lower leg in two places!

"When Doubt Filled My Mind..."

Now, with my father in the hospital, Jesse Jr. away in the army, and her next oldest son, Griffin, hospitalized with a broken leg, Mama wondered, "When will the rain stop pouring?" and How can we tend and harvest all the crops and care for the animals?" "Will we become homeless if we can't manage this farm?" "Will Helena and Louetta have to leave college?"

"I Cried Out, 'I am Slipping!'

Every morning, mama got up before daybreak and went into the coldest room in the house to have a conversation with God. At church, she rejoiced and danced as if all was well, despite some weak comforters, saying things like, *"Well, when it rains it pours!"* We preferred to think of it as a temporary shower.

"But your unfailing love, O LORD, supported me."

For a time, it looked as if those weak comforters may have been right, and the sun would never shine on our family again. Then, one night in late August, as we worked in the packhouse, it appeared that the dam was going to burst! The tears Mama had held back for so long began to well up. It would have been a cathartic release, but at that moment, the door flew open, the toe of a black shoe hit the threshold, and a uniformed soldier appeared in the doorway and swooped her into his arms. Jesse Jr. had been granted a 90-day furlough just as he was about to be deployed overseas.

Your Comfort Gave Renewed Hope and Cheer!

In the middle of our darkest night, a golden ray of hope shone like sunlight! Jesse Jr. took over running the farm. Helena and Louetta stayed in college, and the next spring, my father was discharged from the hospital! Mama's daily morning prayers in the cold room had not been in vain! For a while, the shower had been long and steady, but it was only temporary!

Granny's faith in giving her blessing to Jesse and Lillie Belle's marriage and the faith my mama displayed in constantly praying and dancing through her pain now live in me. And this same faith will work in any difficult situation! With sincere faith, like **Mama's**, a golden ray of hope will break through when you least expect it.

Nine
Promises

My father's relentless teaching flowed into me like oxygen. He and my mother fed our souls on the promises of Psalm 37.

> *"Trust in the LORD and do good, dwell in the land, and feed on His faithfulness. Delight yourself also in the LORD, and He shall give you the desires of your heart."*
> Ps 37:3-4 NKJV

Despite our lower-class status as sharecroppers, navigating the hardships and ugliness of a racist society, my parents believed we would be rewarded for doing good. So, we consumed a steady diet of the promises of that passage.

Prejudiced Christians
The authenticity and power of my parents' faith, hope, and love were protective shields around us. Their unwavering faith provided the foundation on which we could build our future. Their resounding

hope gave us a picture of our future. And their intense love for us and the God who gave us to them produced the stamina to endure the pressures of our racist environment.

As a young man, one of the strangest phenomena I experienced was prejudiced "Christians." For instance, when our family friend, Elder Bolton, was a new convert, "sold out" to the LORD, and still somewhat green, she thought as I did that since the term Christian implies being like Christ, a professed Christian would not disparage people because of their skin color. She was in for a rude awakening!

Carrie was a high school classmate of my sister Gwendolyn, who shared her faith with her when they were attending Livingstone College. She later accepted Christ, joined our church, was called into the ministry, and became a dynamic evangelist. She led most of her family and many others to accept Christ, and most of them joined Royal Light.

One night, Carrie and some friends visited a white Holiness church in Enfield pastored by a man my father knew well. He considered himself a friend and had visited our home. The pastor was apparently a bit shocked when they entered the church. and Startled to see black people coming into a white church, he announced to the congregation, **"Well look at this. God can even save colored folks!"** Being Black, in the pastor's view, must have been one of the worst sins ever! You might imagine the surprise and discomfort her group of recent converts felt.

That incident did not surprise my father, who had interacted with prejudiced "Christians" for some time. In expressing his respect for my father, one white Christian neighbor remarked gleefully, *"Jesse, you are one of the best men I know! I believe God is going to have a special reward for you in heaven. I wouldn't be surprised if He made you the head waiter!"*

In his book, *Jesus and the Disinherited*, Howard Thurman discusses the origin of the slave composition, "I Got Shoes." "*Everybody talking 'bout heav'n ain't going there*" is a line from the Song. A perplexed slave endures ill-treatment from a master who attends church every Sunday. His family wore fine clothing and shoes, and the barefoot, ragged, poorly-clothed slave was required to attend and listen to sermons from the master's preacher. The slave wonders how both he and the master are going to heaven and whether there are two heavens. This idea, however, makes no sense to him as he cannot fathom a just God condoning the master's cruel behavior. He pondered this dilemma throughout the night. The next day, while working in the field, a light bulb goes off in his head. He chuckles to himself, "I've got it!" and composes and sings this spiritual while nodding to his fellow slaves:

I got shoes; you got shoes;
All God's chillun got shoes.
When we get to heav'n we gonna put on our shoes
And shout all over God's heav'n! Heav'n, Heav'n

I got a robe; you got a robe;
all God's chillun got a robe.
When we get to heav'n we gonna put on our robes
And shout all over God's heav'n! Heav'n, heav'n

Then the barefoot slave, in ragged clothes, casts a glance toward the plantation house and adds):

Everybody talking 'bout heav'n ain't goin' there, heav'n...

Our forebears were much wiser than their masters knew. As Ray Allen Billington insists, "[b] y developing this symbolism as a universal language among themselves, they were able to harbor and express thoughts that were not understandable to others," For they understood, as Paul said,

"*The Kingdom of God is not just a lot of talk. It is living by God's power.*" 1 Cor 4:20 NLT

Indeed, "everybody talking about heaven ain't going there." There must be a lifestyle to back up the talk—a lifestyle that exhibits a Christlike attitude that respects the worth of every human being and appreciates that we are all made in the image of God.

Although my family had almost no material wealth, we knew we were made in the image and likeness of God and that, in time, He would give us the desires of our hearts. So, surrounded by God's love and our parents' encouragement, we waited patiently in our cozy, weather-worn farmhouse, where we gathered nightly in the room we affectionately referred to as "the House" for Bible reading and prayer.

The House

To my young mind, Daddy's frequent insistence on gathering us as a family to read the scriptures and pray felt excessive, for my heart was filled with many other desires. I wanted to have a radio show like my cousin, Joe Louis, whose majestic voice I heard on the radio in Daddy and Mama's bedroom. "The House" was where, as a toddler, I sat in front of the fireplace as Daddy read John Bunyan's *Pilgrim's Progress* to me. I did not know that this book was used by abolitionists who saw similarities between the plight of Christian, the main character, and the slave who sought to escape the burden of forced labor and acquire his freedom. Just as Christian faced obstacles and dangers on his journey to the Celestial City, slaves encountered perils and challenges in their quest for emancipation. Both narratives highlight the arduous path from bondage to freedom, whether spiritual or physical.

When Daddy gathered the family in "The House," to

read Scriptures and pray, our parents' wisdom, love, and protection anchored us in this safe place where the desires of my heart began to take root. And Daddy admonished us that if we would delight in the LORD, they would, one day, be ours. He demonstrated that this meant spending time with God, getting to know Him, and learning to really love Him.

I could not have imagined how God was going to grant my desire to host a radio program. But at about seventeen years of age, I began visiting the local gospel station and assisting gospel singer Bill Battle with his fifteen-minute Sunday morning show, and occasionally doing announcements.

Within another five years, I met and became friends with Shirley Caesar, the first black gospel artist to win a Grammy for her version of "Put Your Hand in the Hand." Though Anne Murray and Elvis Presley had previously recorded the song, it was Caesar's soulful, spirited rendition that won a Grammy. She would go on to win eleven more Grammys, including one for lifetime achievement.

When she began hosting her Sunday Morning show, "The Electrifying Evangelist, Shirley Caesar" invited me to co-host "The Moment of Truth" on WSRC in Durham. Though I had heard her as she sang with the Caravans of Chicago and the Caesar Singers, I never imagined meeting her. And now I was co-hosting a radio show with the woman who had been among those featured on Hunter's program! She proved to be one of the kindest, most down-to-earth, people-oriented individuals I have known in life. Although she would subsequently win multiple Grammy, Stellar, and Dove awards, perform at the White House, do cameo movie appearances, and even receive a star on Hollywood Boulevard, she has remained humble. Preferring to avoid the label of "star," she often remarked, "If you spell 'star' backward, you get 'rats!'

After four years of co-hosting, I was offered my own three-hour Sunday morning gospel program on a new Durham station, WDUR/WFXC AM/FM. That program was simulcast on Cablevision and after a couple of years, it expanded to six hours. Daddy had gone to be with the Lord a year earlier, but his demonstration of love for God was at work in me! His and Mama's constant refrain, "Delight thyself in the Lord, and he will give you the desires of your heart" resounded in my memory as I was confidently standing on the promises of God!

Some of my heart's desires might seem inconsequential. For example, when entering department stores to browse for clothing and other items, I frequently encountered white clerks who approached me with a skeptical tone, asking, "Can I help you?" Their demeanor and inflection clearly conveyed an air of cynicism and suspicion. If I responded that I just wanted to look around, the clerk followed me, watching suspiciously. This sparked my desire to work in retail so I could treat everyone the way I wanted to be treated. When the Sears store several miles from campus, hired me, I didn't have a car and had to secure transportation from a variety of sources. Yet, my transportation was almost like the prophet Elijah's experience when, at God's command, "the ravens brought him bread and meat each morning and evening" (1 Kgs 17:6). God fulfilled my desire to work in retail and provided transportation.

I wanted to sing professionally, and Evangelist Shirley Caesar allowed the little boy from the Slashes Lowlands to travel with and occasionally fill in with the Caesar Singers. What a thrilling experience! A couple of years earlier, she invited me to accompany her group to play guitar on a weekend tour to New York City and Hartford, Connecticut. She had heard me as I was playing around with the guitar one night in her mother's living room, and since her regular guitarist, James Simpson, was unavailable, she invited me to fill in. After rehearsing with the group just once, I felt nervous and out of my league, and my performance clearly underwhelmed Miss Caesar. A guitarist for the renowned gospel group, The Five Blind Boys, was visiting, so she suggested I receive a few pointers from him. As he picked up the instrument and started playing intricate riffs, fear of failure overtook me, and I knew I would not be playing on that tour! Fortunately, my confidence grew over time and two years later. I was invited to fill in for background singer, Suella Colbert, who could not make who was unable to make a tour to South Carolina and Georgia.

By then, I had completed undergraduate school and was teaching high school in Durham. After several years of teaching, my first administrative position was as an assistant principal for a prestigious public high school, Walt Whitman, in Maryland. I was one of only three administrators and the first African American assistant principal at the school in an affluent suburb of Washington, DC. Some years later, God granted me the desire to become a principal at a middle school in the same suburb.

How appropriate that the school's mascot was the Phoenix. This bird soars as it rises from the ashes. And much like this mythical creature, I had risen from a poor black community, the Slashes, and had become the principal of a top-level school in a well-to-do, predominantly white community. Though I knew I would succeed by trusting God and standing on His promises, "the howling storms of doubt and fear" soon began to assail me.

As I weathered some strong storms, I wanted to serve at least four or five years as principal. Meanwhile, I implemented several successful programs, including an annual retreat of the Instructional Council, which became the Instructional Leadership Team. At the first six-hour Saturday retreat, which took place in the basement of my home, we developed the C. A. R. E. project. The acronym stood for Communication, Accountability, Responsibility, and Environment. It signaled that everyone would be expected to **c**ommunicate respectfully and responsibly and be **a**ccountable for their actions to colleagues, students, and each other. It was also everyone's **r**esponsibility to help make the school safe, warm, welcoming, successful, and take care of the **e**nvironment to keep our school clean.

The C. A. R. E. project underscored the reason I wanted to become a principal. I desired to lead a caring school environment in which everyone felt valued. That ideology carried through for the fifteen years I led the school. And, all that time, I was standing on God's faithful **promises**!

Ten
Love

"Such love has no fear, because perfect love expels all fear. If we are afraid, it is for fear of punishment, and this shows that we have not fully experienced his perfect love."

1 John 4:18 NLT

For some, it may seem that I accomplished a lot. Yet, I stopped far short of following up on many opportunities because I did not understand the power of perfect love to set me free. I often allowed myself to be trapped behind many self-imposed barriers.

My participation in the 1960s' school desegregation experiment was indeed daring. Yet, five years after enrolling in Enfield Graded School, where I was initially treated as a social pariah, I was elected vice president of the student council at Enfield High. The following year, I was elected president of the student council. By then the black high school, T. S. Inborden, had been closed and its students sent to Enfield High. In an atmosphere fraught with fear, uncertainty, and tenuous race relations, I felt a strong sense of obligation mixed with inadequacy and fear. If it were not for the strong encouragement of my parents, as well as student friends and teachers who believed in me and pushed me forward, I would not have persisted.

During my high school senior year, the Twenty-sixth Amendment to the Constitution granting voting rights to 18-year-olds had been ratified and I organized what was likely the first voter registration drive for 18-year-olds in North Carolina. Subsequently, I was contacted by representatives of Chapel Hill, North Carolina mayor, Howard Lee, the first and only black mayor of that university town, who was putting together a campaign to run for governor; his team wanted me to lead the youth division. Like Moses, when God called him to confront Pharaoh on behalf of the Hebrew slaves, I gave a plethora of excuses. A strong, unfounded sense of inadequacy convinced me I was not up to it.

Certainly, I supported the mayor's campaign as a monumental step in advancing equitable justice for the state's black community. I also relished the prospect of someone who looked like me becoming the governor of North Carolina. But I feared that my incompetence would be exposed. So once more, *low self-esteem and self-imposed mental barriers* led to a missed opportunity to commit to a leadership role. Like the chicken and pig analogy, I did not mind contributing but was unwilling to commit. And this was another clear case of *imperfect love*.

When the black citizens of Enfield, Halifax, and Scotland Neck, North Carolina, organized the Neighborhood Action Committee during my senior year in high school, I was nominated to serve as president. Though I protested, the nominators refused to withdraw my name. So, I begged the attendees not to vote for me! Still I received the second-highest number of votes and was forced to assume the position of vice president.

Sometime later, I sensed that the committee was focused more on social events than justice and felt powerless to make a difference. So rather than fight to steer my colleagues back on course as Orville Wright must have done when his brother veered off mission, I quit. I regret that action to this day and realize that it reflected *imperfect love*. I did not *love* my community enough to stay in the fight.

As I was completing my master's degree at North Carolina Central University, Dr. Stephen Fortune, a noted professor, saw academic potential in me and offered to assist me in getting into a doctoral program at Duke University. Although I had done most of the research for my master's thesis in its libraries and traversed the campus to the point that I was quite comfortable there, my self-image was too small to envision getting a PhD from that prestigious institution. So, I declined his offer. Imagine the positive impact I could have made on other young minds trapped in low-level thinking like mine! Imagine—if only I had seized that opportunity to pave a path for them to emerge from the confines of fear! *Imperfect love* had subtly won again!

Though several people suggested that I become a principal, I remained in the classroom for 20 years before entering school administration. Similarly, after having my call to the ministry confirmed repeatedly, decades passed before I acted on it. Though others saw it, I could not envision what God had deposited in a little barefoot boy from the Slashes Lowlands. Even now, I recall the time Evangelist Hunter saw a light on my forehead and asked others who were standing near me if they could see it. Her surprising words are still with me, "Can't you all see that light in his forehead? It is so bright!" What I did not understand then but now understand is that God was beginning to unveil his purpose for my life and ministry. It was the purpose that had been planted in me early and watered by the gift of a little silver trumpet from my father one night before the dawning of Christmas day. I was to use my voice like a trumpet to make an impact in the earth.

With the passing of time, I have come to see barriers as tactics of the devil, who is not only a liar but the father of lies. He uses them to inflict the spirit of fear on the believer! I now know that what appeared impenetrable had already been severed for me!

"For He has broken the gates of bronze and cut the bars of iron in two." Ps 107:16 NKJV

Although the barriers confining my family within the sharecropping system **were as real** as the chains that held Peter in jail, but fell off when the angel of the Lord awakened him. I only needed to press on by faith. I have discovered what my father already knew, that though they were real they had also been **severed**!

In our journey through life, we often encounter what seem like impenetrable obstacles. While some would have us believe otherwise, these barriers, once as formidable as bronze gates with iron bars, now stand severed and ineffective. These self-appointed gatekeepers, who attempt to deny us access and shut us out, are merely guarding ruins. And though they threaten to try to impede our progress, their power is an illusion. Their gates are already breached, and their bars severed. Though they threaten to discourage us with paralyzing fear, we have a greater source of strength.

With Daddy's encouragement, I came to understand that our task is simply to keep moving onward and upward. God's divine hand has already broken these barriers for us. This realization manifests itself as pure, powerful, and perfect love that propels us beyond the illusion of limitation and into the realm of infinite possibility. In the end, the only true barriers are those we allow to exist in our minds. We can overcome any obstacle in our path with faith, perseverance, and perfect **love.**

Conclusion

From Tormenting Fear to Perfect Love

Reflecting on my life's journey, I allowed fear and imperfect love to rob me of golden opportunities. Could it be that the hitchhiking angel was not at all a fantasy? I do not know if I will ever have a face-to-face encounter with an angel, but I am no longer tormented by fear. Perhaps fear prevented me from having the opportunity for an epiphany like Zechariah with a genuine heavenly visitor bringing glad tidings.

The spirit of fear is paralyzing! It does not align with God's offering of power, love, and a sound mind (2 Tim 1:7). Though Jesus did not want to experience the agony of the cross, He was not tormented, dissuaded nor paralyzed by fear. Because he was filled with perfect love for the Father and guided by his love for the people for whom He gave His life.

Now, when God presents me with opportunities, I understand that failure to pursue them reflects not only a lack of faith in my abilities but *imperfect love* for God and those who could benefit from my pursuit of them. So, I go after them with abandon.

When offered the opportunity to pursue the position of principal of a largely white middle school in an affluent community, I did not hesitate to go after it despite being a black man with a background in an impoverished community. When I arrived at the school, white and Asian students were soaring academically, but black and brown students were falling substantially behind. Perfect love for these students caused me to fight to raise their achievement levels and challenge my staff to use new methods to attempt to close the gap.

Like the mascot, I had risen from the deadness of the Slashes to new life in a challenging yet exciting position with faith and love rather than a spirit of fear. My black and brown students' academic levels increased significantly during my tenure as principal. My staff demonstrated a greater understanding of race, equity, and the influence of cultural differences on teaching and learning. Armed with perfect love, I completed a Doctor of Ministry degree, writing my dissertation on my work to close the achievement gap.

In his letter to his young colleague, the apostle Paul admonished Timothy,

"God has not given us the spirit of fear; but of power, and of love, and of a sound mind" (2 Tim 1:7 KJV).

Earlier, I speculated about how Zechariah's outcome might have been different if he had succumbed to fear and fled from the temple. But what if the hitchhiking angel I feared in my teenage years had in fact, been the Angel of the LORD. What if that angel had been Immanuel, Yeshua, the stranger the two disciples met on the Emmaus Road, or the One Paul encountered on the road to Damascus? My tormenting fear may have caused me to miss a life-transforming opportunity!

But thank God, I love Him more perfectly now. The Apostle John stated it best.

> *"There is no fear in love; but perfect love casts out fear because fear involves torment. But he who fears has not been made perfect in love."*
>
> 1Jn 4:18 NKJV

Like my brother Jesse, we must love people enough to work until God calls us home. Instead of allowing past unpleasant, painful, or sinful experiences to fill us with melancholy and despair, we should recognize God's hand working to teach, develop, and transform us. By doing so, we can reach our full potential in Christ and become a source of blessing to others around us. For when we are filled with God's love, we are at peace both in our own spirit and with everyone else.

Through it all, I have come to realize that our life experiences are not meant solely for us. Each of us has a responsibility to live, love, and share what we've learned so that the lessons we gain also benefit others. Until my work is complete, also like my big brother, Jesse Jr., I will remain faithful to the mission and never stop **standing on the promises of God!**

About the Author

Dr. Alton E. Sumner, an inspiring speaker, minister, and author, is an ordained minister and former secondary school principal. Sumner rose from the abject poverty of a remote place called the Slashes Lowlands in eastern North Carolina, navigating the hardships his family experienced as sharecroppers and battling prejudice, discrimination, and racism. After teaching high school and college for 20 years, he became principal of one of the nation's leading academic middle schools and spent over two decades in that capacity. He promoted educational salvation, social justice, and cultural and racial understanding. In addition, he had an exciting advocation as a radio and television host in the Research Triangle area for some thirteen years.

Dr. Sumner holds Bachelor's and Master of Arts degrees in history and a Doctor of Ministry degree in strategic leadership. Presently, Sumner teaches biblical studies at Calvary Bible Institute. He is married to his loving wife of more than three decades, Betty, and is the father of two amazing adult children, Jonathan and Nichelle.

www.ingramcontent.com/pod-product-compliance
Lightning Source LLC
Chambersburg PA
CBHW070119080526
44586CB00013B/1338